PARKER AND THE CITY IN THE SEA
A Play
By Ian August

Uproar Theatrics

LICENSING & PRODUCTION INQUIRIES
Uproar Theatrics, LLC.
hello@uproartheatrics.com | www.UproarTheatrics.com

Parker and the City in the Sea copyright © 2021 by Ian August

Parker and the City in the Sea is published by Uproar Theatrics, LLC
500 8th Ave FRNT 3, #1714 New York, NY 10018

ISBN: 978-1-968051-27-3

First Printing, April 2025

Parker and the City in the Sea

Cast of Characters:

Parker – Colleen's brother, 17, Male, brave undersea explorer and introverted high-schooler

Colleen – Parker's sister, 17, Female, hard-ass. She walks with arm braces due to an accident in Junior High

Grace – New Girl in school, 17, Female, demure, a little shy, good student

Jessie (or Jesse) – Classmate, 17, F/M, the Alpha-dog, doesn't work well with others

Pat (Patrick or Patricia) – Classmate, 17, M/F, friend of Jessie's, not the brightest bulb

Doug – Research scientist, Male, 30s, submersible engineer, perpetually grumpy

Judy – Research scientist, Female, late 20s, marine anthropologist, cheerful and optimistic

Henson – School Counselor, Adult, M/F, over-enthusiastic

Briggs – School Principal, Adult, M/F, brusque, direct

Tennyson – English Teacher, Adult, M/F, gentle, passionate, empathetic

Anker – Social Services, Adult, M/F, all business, no fun

Place:
In and around an unnamed high school and also the ocean floor

Time:
Present Day

<u>Notes on Casting:</u>

Any gender identifiers for the M/F characters in the body of the script are irrelevant, and should be determined solely by the director in production.

If the cast is limited to ten actors, the role of Anker can be played by the actors who play Judy and Doug, either individually or in tandem.

<u>Additional Notes from the Playwright:</u>

A note on the language: There are a few obscenities sprinkled throughout the script. If those words will disturb or upset your audience, feel free to reach out to Uproar for alternative terms.

A note on PAT: If the role of PAT is to be played by a male actor, please replace the "Patricia Lee" monologue on Page 41 with the following:

> It's Pat. Actually, it's Patrick. Actually, it's Patrick Lee, but no one calls me Patrick Lee except my mom, and I hate it, so I usually just go by Pat. Or Patrick. No one ever calls me "Trick."

PARKER AND THE CITY IN THE SEA was originally produced at the 2018 Edinburgh Festival Fringe in Edinburgh, Scotland, in association with the American High School Theatre Festival, and featuring students from The Lawrenceville School. Directed by Matthew R. Campbell. Production Design by Matthew R. Campbell; Lighting Design by James Cuthrell; Company Manager Karla Guido. The original cast was as follows:

Parker - Casey Rogerson
Colleen - Bailey Foltz
Grace - Maggie Ross
Jesse - Daniel Irvine
Pat - Deven Kinney
Judy - Adelaide "Addi" Brown
Doug - Simon Cull
Henson - Nicholas Winkler
Briggs - Owen Bird
Tennyson - Winston Shum
Anker - Addi Brown / Simon Cull

Tech Crew - Anushka Agarwala, Emily Macham, Kieran Pierre

PARKER AND THE CITY IN THE SEA

1.

In the darkness, a ping. Repeating slowly. A few pings, and then the sounds of water, like the inside of water—muffled, deep. A light comes up center stage revealing PARKER, 17, hair tousled, lanky, in goggles. There is a determined look on his face. There is a backpack on his lap. It has seen better days.

PARKER:

Down and down and down we go.

As the light becomes brighter, we see that PARKER is seated in a small globular pod, staring out into the darkness.

What will we find? Nobody knows.

He presses a button above him, activating a voice recorder.

We are... 3300 feet below the surface of the Pacific, two hundred miles east of the island of Panay, northeast Indonesia. Right now everything is calm, and the only sounds are the pings of the sonar guidance systems, and the only movements are the lumbering of great aquatic beasts that undulate through the static depths of the sea.
Initiating sonar sweep.

A voice cuts through the ocean.

JUDY:

Parker? Parker—come in, please.

PARKER:

Hey Judy.

> *JUDY appears in her own light, a woman in her
> late twenties, off to the side. She wears a life
> jacket and rain gear, glasses, a cap to shield her
> from the sun. She holds an electronic tablet.*

JUDY:

Lost you for a second. It gave me quite a scare.

PARKER:

Didn't mean to spook you. How's the weather holding up?

> *In another light across the stage, DOUG
> appears—thirties, gruff. He wears a life jacket
> as well, and a knit cap. He is not thrilled to be
> there.*

DOUG:

I didn't build a five million dollar submarine so you could ask us about the weather.

JUDY:

It's fine. Blue skies, 72 degrees. There looks to be a small storm system coming in from the east, but it's nothing we haven't been through before.

PARKER:

How strong is it?

DOUG:

Strong enough for me to wish I was still in bed.

JUDY:

Quiet, Doug.

DOUG:

With a warm book and a good cup of coffee. But *nooo*...

JUDY:

(*to PARKER*) I'm getting the results of the sonar—look to your left.

> *Long shadows stretch up from the floor; bursts of bubbles and the whoosh of air.*

PARKER:

Hydrothermal vents. These giant black volcanic towers are everywhere.

JUDY:

Keep your distance, please—

DOUG:

If you wreck Petunia, I'll break your neck.

PARKER:

(*amused*) Understood. I'll be careful.

> *A wave of pink lights move past, and PARKER's eyes excitedly follow it.*

Wow!

JUDY:

Parker? Are you okay?

PARKER:

Jellyfish—seventy—maybe eighty strong.

JUDY:

Pacific sea nettles?

PARKER:

Yeah, pink and orange and yellow... and it looks—oh, ho!

A vast shadow follows in the same direction of the lights, rolling over PARKER and then vanishing.

JUDY:

What? What is it?

PARKER:

A six-gilled shark. Ten feet long or so? A little one.

DOUG:

It's practically a guppy.

JUDY:

Quiet, Doug. The video camera's rolling, right?

PARKER:

Of course it is—

JUDY:

I'll upload the feed now.

DOUG:

Parker—the storm is moving in, you need to focus.

PARKER:

You're right, of course.

DOUG:

Because I want you and Petunia back to the surface as soon as possible.

PARKER:

I don't know how long it will take, Doug—

JUDY:

Take as long as you need.

DOUG:

Don't take as long as you need. I can feel my hair turning gray as we speak.

JUDY:

I like gray hair.

PARKER:

It all depends on what we find.

JUDY:

Well, you only have about seventy hours of oxygen left, so let that be a guideline.

PARKER:

More than enough.

> *PARKER engages the thrusters, there is a whoosh of water and a gentle hum of engines.*

DOUG:

I don't know why I agreed to this stupid idea in the first place.

JUDY:

I'm terribly convincing.

DOUG:

You're a pain in my butt.

> *The submarine pings.*

PARKER:

Doug—that old fisherman in Manila said it was here, that the lost city was here. And if he's right, if local legends are correct—

DOUG:

Local legends are never correct, Park. That's why they're legends.

JUDY:

Oh, God. Remember that time we spent stuck in a coral reef off the coast of Chile?

DOUG:

Judy...

JUDY:

Or that time you banked on those rocks in the Mozambique Channel! Hah!

DOUG:

Judy!

JUDY:

What?

Ping!

DOUG:

Parker... come back to the surface. This is ridiculous.

PARKER:

Maybe. But it's just a few hundred feet before I reach the ocean floor. A few hundred feet until I finally see what I've been searching for. What greater men than I have sought for hundreds and hundreds of years.

Beat. He takes a deep breath.
                    PARKER (cont):
The lost city of Atlantis.

                    DOUG:
You're so dramatic.

> *A bell rings—a school bell, cutting like a scream through the ocean. PARKER's eyes widen as the world around him—the sea, Petunia, JUDY and DOUG—vanishes. He is left standing in the middle of a High School hallway. He looks terrified.*
>
> *Beat.*
>
> *PARKER runs off stage.*

2.

> *A classroom in the school. TENNYSON, an English professor whose colorful bow tie betrays the soul of an artist, lectures the students seated in the room—JESSIE, PAT, and GRACE, all 17 years old. JESSIE is the model of contemporary coolness; PAT appears to emulate his friend, but with less success; GRACE is far more subdued, almost conservative, confident. She is not quite allied with them, but not quite not. There is a student missing, a single empty chair.*

                    TENNYSON:
"Water, water everywhere / nor any drop to drink." Does anybody know what that's from?
The Rime of the Ancient Mariner. The longest poem Samuel Taylor Coleridge wrote, inspired by the exploratory voyages

TENNYSON (cont):
of James Cook throughout the Pacific. The poem tells the story of a sailor who confronts a man on his way to a wedding and forces him to hear his adventures. The man, known as the "wedding guest," eventually becomes fascinated by the dramatic, fantastical exploits of the sailor, and listens to the whole thing. It's a remarkable piece of literature, and also a very important one: The poem was the jumping off point for the English Romantic poetic movement in the early 19th century.
Can anybody name other Romantic poets?
Jessie? How about you?

JESSIE:
Um, Jay-Z?

TENNYSON:
I don't think so.
Pat? Any ideas?

PAT:
Who wrote, "roses are red and violets are blue?"

TENNYSON:
It's from a nursery rhyme.

PAT:
That guy?

PAT stares at TENNYSON blankly.

GRACE:
Wordsworth?

TENNYSON:
Very good, Grace. Yes, Wordsworth. Keats, Byron, Shelley. William Blake.

JESSIE:

(*beneath her breath*) Yeah, *very good* Grace.

PAT turns to JESSIE.

PAT:

I'm Pat.

JESSIE:

I was talking to *her*, Pat.

PAT:

Oh. Right.

TENNYSON:

I like when my new students step it up.
So here's what I'd like you all to do for homework tonight.
Take a moment to read part one of *The Rime of the Ancient
Mariner*, and then follow it up by reading at least one poem
of Wordsworth, Byron, or Shelley. Try to find what
similarities they have stylistically. And then let's figure out
what Romanticism actually *is* in relation to—

> *COLLEEN enters. She is on arm crutches. Her
> face is a stony mask of defiance, a fractured dam
> holding back a deluge. She moves to the empty
> seat, and sits down heavily in it. Everyone
> watches her. COLLEEN does not give a damn.*

Nice of you to join us, Colleen.

COLLEEN:

Thanks.

TENNYSON:
When we only have five minutes left in class. Would you mind telling me where you've been?

COLLEEN:
The bathroom.

TENNYSON:
For forty minutes?

COLLEEN:
I really had to go.

JESSIE and PAT giggle.

TENNYSON:
I don't think that's very funny.

COLLEEN:
I'll work on my act.

TENNYSON:
I'll need to see you after class, then.

COLLEEN:
Can't. Busy.

TENNYSON:
Doing what?

COLLEEN:
Cutting pre-calc.

JESSIE and PAT giggle again. TENNYSON sighs.

TENNYSON:
Do you at least have your textbook?

COLLEEN:
No.

TENNYSON:
You left it at home again?

COLLEEN locks eyes with TENNYSON.

COLLEEN:
I burned it.

Beat.

TENNYSON:
Shall we go see Principal Briggs?

COLLEEN:
Yes. We shall.

COLLEEN stands with the help of her arm crutches.

TENNYSON:
(*to the class, a little shaken*) I'll be right back. Please read the first part of the... of the... thing I asked you to read. The homework.

PAT:
We're not at home.

TENNYSON:
That's a great observation, Pat. We'll discuss... when I get back.

TENNYSON and COLLEEN exit.

Beat.

JESSIE:

That was hilarious.

GRACE:

Who was that?

JESSIE:

That was Colleen.

PAT:

She is going to be in sooooo much trouble.

JESSIE:

Please. They let her get away with everything. Like that time when Leo started dating Camila, but he totally still had that thing for Kate and everyone was like, whatever Leo. That's Colleen. Whatever Colleen.

PAT:

I have a thing for cake.

JESSIE:

Kate, Pat. Jeez.

PAT

Oh yeah. My bad.

GRACE:

But Colleen—she missed the whole class.

JESSIE:

Colleen's a pity case.

PAT:

They never do anything to her.

GRACE:

Why not?

JESSIE:

They feel bad for her. Ever since the accident, Colleen's been coasting on those crutches.

GRACE:

What accident?

PAT:

She broke her back.

JESSIE:

Stepped on a crack, I guess.

PAT:

A crack on her roof, right?

JESSIE:

It's an expression, Pat. Jeez. Run into walls head-first much?

PAT:

How much is much?

GRACE:

She fell off her roof? Wow!

PAT:

Wow yeah. She was in a wheelchair through almost all of freshman year.

JESSIE:
Colleen's a bitch. She was one before the accident, and she's one now.

PAT:
We used to be friends.

JESSIE:
Until she came for you.

PAT:
My mom came for me. To bring me home.

JESSIE:
She threw you out of her house!

PAT:
I spilled some juice.

GRACE:
That's some bad day.

PAT:
It *was* everywhere. And it was purple.

JESSIE:
Look Grace, you're new—let me give you some advice. Stay away from Colleen. She's got more issues than *French Vogue*.

GRACE:
Okay.

JESSIE:
Better yet: stay away from the whole screwed-up family.

GRACE:

Family?

JESSIE:

Colleen's a twin.

PAT:

Her brother Parker—

JESSIE:
Parker's a nut job. He's out of his mind.

PAT:
They were raised by their grandparents.

JESSIE:
Dad travels for work or something. And the mom is out of the picture. She's probably the smartest one in the bunch.

PAT:

Colleen's pretty smart.

JESSIE:
You know what I mean, Pat.

GRACE:
So what's wrong with the brother? With Parker?

PAT:

He sees things.

JESSIE:
Parker has hallucinations.

PAT:

Like, all the time.

JESSIE:
Another hot mess.

GRACE:
He has hallucinations? About what?

JESSIE:
Either one of them could snap at a moment's notice. Like
Solange in an elevator.

PAT:
Yeah.

JESSIE:
You have no idea what I'm talking about, do you?

PAT snaps her fingers. She does not.

Nice meeting you, Grace. But you're better off forgetting
they even exist.

The bell rings.

3.

*The office of MS. HENSON, the school
Guidance Counselor, who tries too hard and
stares too long. A clock ticks like a metronome in
the background. The office is painfully silent.
PARKER sits across from MS. HENSON, at the
desk. PARKER's head is down. HENSON stares
at him like he's a lost puppy.*

HENSON:
Mr. Cleary found you in the hallway again.

Beat.

That's the third time this month, Parker.

Beat.

You know, I used to daydream a lot at school. I would imagine the wildest things—things that would make your head spin. Like, I would imagine I was outside, playing on the playground. Or sometimes I was having ice cream with my friends. Have you ever? Ha ha! My teachers used to yell at me and give me detention, but it did no good. My parents had to explain to my teachers that I had an over-active imagination. But the next day, I'd be staring off into space, dreaming about reading a book! I was incorrigible! I know you daydream too, Parker. I've spoken to your teachers about it, and they understand.

PARKER:
I don't daydream.

HENSON:
Don't you, Park? Can I call you Park?

PARKER:
No.

Beat.

How are things at home, Parker?
Is there something that happened at home, Parker?
Something else that happened?

Beat.

What about your sister? How is she doing?

*PARKER's head pops up. Across the stage, lights
come up on the office of PRINCIPAL BRIGGS.
He paces behind the desk, frustrated. COLLEEN
sits in the chair facing BRIGGS, the back of her
chair touches the back of PARKER's chair.
HENSON and PARKER remain in the light.*

BRIGGS:
I'm about at the end of my tether with you, Colleen.

HENSON:
It *is* about Colleen, isn't it?

BRIGGS:
We all are. And Mr. Tennyson is not an easy man to upset.

COLLEEN:
I've been practicing.

HENSON:
Take your time, Parker. Tell me what happened with Colleen.

BRIGGS:
I think we—the administration and I—have tried our hardest
to do everything we can for you and your brother. But you're
cutting classes, you're disrespecting teachers, you're
disappearing altogether. We're concerned about you.

COLLEEN:
At least someone is.

BRIGGS:
Is your dad still abroad?

COLLEEN:
No, he's hiding in the basement.

BRIGGS:
A simple yes or no would suffice.
Look, you've gone from an A student to barely passing—and
you're smart. God knows, you're smart. You won the
Science Fair competition freshman year, for goodness sake.
That's unheard of.

COLLEEN:
Thank you.

BRIGGS:
But I am quickly running out of options for you, young lady.
And sending you back to Ms. Henson doesn't seem like it
would do either of you any good.

HENSON:
Parker? Will you say something?

COLLEEN:
Ms. Henson is an idiot.

BRIGGS:
Ms. Henson is a qualified educational therapist—

COLLEEN:
Ms. Henson is convinced I'm the spawn of Satan.

HENSON:
Did Colleen... hurt you?

COLLEEN:
She's an absolute moron.

HENSON:
Because if she did...

PARKER:
(*quickly*) She would never hurt me.

BRIGGS:
Okay. I will tell Ms. Henson to lay off.

COLLEEN:
Lay off me, and lay off my brother.

HENSON:
Are you sure?

BRIGGS:
Deal. But you need to do something for me, Colleen. You need to figure out what you want out of... this. Out of school. Out of life.

HENSON:
You know you can tell me anything, Parker.

BRIGGS:
Once you do—I promise I will help you figure out how to get it.

HENSON:
Because if you don't...

BRIGGS:
Because if you don't,

BRIGGS and HENSON:
I won't be able to help you at all.

HENSON:
It's my job, as your guidance counselor, to recommend what's best for you.

BRIGGS:

Understand?

HENSON:

Parker?

COLLEEN:

Capiche.

PARKER grabs his bag, and rushes out.

HENSON begins taking notes.

BRIGGS:

Remember, Colleen—at some point it's out of my control.
Don't let it get to that point.

Beat.

COLLEEN:

I won't.

4.

JUDY appears in the darkness.

JUDY:

According to Plato, the lost city of Atlantis was once an
island populated by a noble and generous race of people. The
island was beautiful and filled with natural resources, and
the people of the island became wealthy and happy in their
lives.

Lights rise on DOUG, across the stage.

DOUG:

Sounds like a crock.

JUDY:

Don't be so grim, Douglas. The stories go on to say how that happiness was corrupted by their greed and power—so much so that they became evil. And the gods of Olympus punished them and sunk the island and the city into the sea.

DOUG:

That's more believable than the first part.

JUDY:

Some Atlanteologans—

DOUG:

"Atlanteologans?"

JUDY:

Yes, Doug. Some Atlanteologans believe that the Atlanteans were the first to create nuclear capabilities. And the wars that they fought resulted in their ultimate demise.

DOUG:

Nuclear capabilities? When was this?

JUDY:

Around 3100BC.

DOUG:

And how, pray tell, were they able to enrich the uranium needed to make these weapons?

JUDY:

Martin Freksa—

DOUG:

Who??

JUDY:

Martin Freksa is a German Atlanteologist. He wrote a book.

DOUG:

Anyone can write a book, Judy. Idiots write books all the time.

JUDY:

Anyway, Freksa thought that the Atlanteans were technologically advanced enough to develop these weapons on their own.

> *Lights rise on PARKER at the helm of Petunia, announced with a ping of sonar.*

PARKER:

What do *you* think, Judy?

JUDY:

I think something existed that Plato wrote about—it's mentioned in both his dialogue with Timaeus and his dialogue with Critius—in pretty significant detail. I find it hard to believe it was purely a morality story about the dangers of hubris.

DOUG:

And that's *your* fatal flaw.

PARKER:

No more talk of fatality, please? It's a little scary when all you can see is black.

DOUG:

Sorry.

JUDY:
How's the air down there?

PARKER:
We're at about 100 atmospheres of pressure and climbing. Seventy kilometers off the coast of Andalusia, about two thousand feet down into the Atlantic. I've got fish and I've got squid, but no sign yet of the Lost City.

DOUG:
And you're not likely to find any.

PARKER:
We just have to find the right place.

DOUG:
It's called the "Lost City" for a reason, Park.

JUDY:
I agree with Parker.

DOUG:
(*interjecting*) You would.

JUDY:
(*ignoring him*) It's not a matter of "if," it's a matter of "when." We have the technology, and we have Plato.

DOUG:
I have a migraine.

PARKER:
I'm coming up on the sea floor, I'm going to activate the aft sensors.

DOUG:

Bring it down slow, Park.

PARKER:

Will do.

> *The lights from Petunia suddenly cast a glow across a bustling sea floor. Scuttling crabs and slithering fish swirl through the sediment, reds and browns, and greens, and grays. The muted sounds of the thrusters firing off, and then the Petunia lurches, steadies.*

Lots of life down here.

DOUG:

Bring home something for dinner.

JUDY:

Ha ha.

PARKER:

I'm going to do another sonar sweep and then we can figure out which direction to head out.

JUDY:

I have a good feeling about this, Parker, I really do.

PARKER:

Me, too.

DOUG:

You two are ridiculous.

JUDY:

Birds of a feather!

Beat.

DOUG:

What happens if you don't find Atlantis here?

PARKER:

We go somewhere else.

DOUG:

And what happens if you don't find it there? I mean, what's your end game, buddy?

> *PARKER goes quiet. Only the sounds of the water, and the movement of Petunia break the silence. The occasional ping from the sonar system.*

JUDY:

(*to PARKER*) We'll find it, sweetie. Don't you worry.

> *PARKER activates the thrusters, and he is surrounded by a swirl of dirt from the sea floor.*
>
> *Behind them, a figure stands in the dark of the ocean, observing.*
>
> *Lights fade on PARKER, JUDY, DOUG, and the ocean floor. They exit. They rise on...*

5.

> *...GRACE, standing behind where PARKER stood in the hallway of the school. She is shocked into a stunned silence.*
>
> *JESSIE and PAT enter, see GRACE.*

JESSIE:

Wow. I mean, just: Wow.

PAT:

He was doing it again?

GRACE:

Yeah.

JESSIE:

Unbelievable, right?

GRACE:

He was just in his own world. Like nothing else existed.

JESSIE:

He's a looney.

PAT:

Like, a bird?

JESSIE:

Like, a *lunatic*, Pat. And so is his sister.

GRACE:

But he wasn't hurting anybody. He was, like, trapped in his imagination. I've never seen anything like that before. It was so... so sad.

JESSIE:

It's not sad. It's pathetic. He obviously needs to go on some sort of meds or something.

PAT:

Once, when I thought I saw a ghost, my mom gave me soup, and I was, like, totally better.

GRACE:
Have you both seen him do this?

JESSIE:
Oh, a ton of times.

Behind them, COLLEEN enters.

Once, he zoned out in the middle of a science lab. We were
dissecting a squid or something horrible, and he just went
blank. Right in the middle of class. I thought Mrs. Burns
didn't know whether to call an ambulance or the nut house.
And then once, during Art class, we were painting, and then
you heard, like, a "ding" or something, and it was him. He
said "ding!" It was all I could do not to burst out laughing in
the middle of class. I painted a straight jacket for him, but he
didn't seem to find that funny.

COLLEEN:
For who?

*JESSIE's mouth snaps shut. COLLEEN
approaches.*

Come on, Jessie. Let it out. Who needs the ambulance? Who
needs a straight jacket?

*There is a brief pause where JESSIE decides
whether or not to engage.*

JESSIE:
Your freak show of a brother, of course.

COLLEEN:
There we go.

PAT:
Grace caught him... seeing stuff.

COLLEEN:
If I were you, I'd be careful about what you say about my brother.

JESSIE:
Are you threatening us?

COLLEEN:
Not yet. But I could change that pretty quick.

PAT:
Don't get mad, Coll. Jessie didn't mean anything by it.

COLLEEN:
Of course not.

PAT:
It was, like, a joke.

COLLEEN:
Ha ha. Some joke.

JESSIE:
It wasn't a joke. Your brother is a disaster, Colleen, and you'd rather hide away on the roof of the school than deal with it.

COLLEEN:
You been spying on me, Jessie? I knew you were obsessed, but that's a little bit much, donchathink?

JESSIE:
Oh, puh-lease. I'm about as obsessed with you as Christina was obsessed with Brittney, which is like, not a bit!

PAT:
Not a Brit?

COLLEEN:
God, Jessie. You're as dumb as I remember.

JESSIE:
Like you're so smart? Then why do you let your brother run around school staring off into space like some alien?

COLLEEN:
He's his own person. He can do what he wants.

JESSIE:
Your brother is a psychotic mess. My mother says that he could have a break at any time and kill one of us. And my mother knows about crazy people. She went to boarding school.

COLLEEN:
Do you want to see which of us will have a psychotic break first, Jessie?

JESSIE:
That was a threat—did you hear that? That was a threat. She threatened me.

GRACE:
Calm down, Jessie.

JESSIE:
You—you're a menace to the school. You and your schitzo brother. You should both be committed. And I won't let you threaten me with... with... your robot arms.

COLLEEN:
They're crutches, you moron. But if you want a real threat,
I'm happy to make one:

PAT:
Colleen—

COLLEEN:
If I ever find you talking to my brother, if I ever hear you
talking about my brother, if I see you even *look* at my
brother, *you're* going to need an ambulance to get the end
of my crutch out of your lower intestine. Do you
understand me? I will shove this crutch so far up your ass
that they will be able to see it touching your tonsils when
you open that fat mouth of yours. And that goes for all of
you dipwads.

JESSIE:
Big words from our resident cripple.

GRACE:
Jessie!

COLLEEN:
Say. That. Again. Jessie.
Come on.
Just say it.
Say it again.

TENNYSON enters.

TENNYSON:
What's going on here?

Beat.

JESSIE:

Nothing, Mr. Tennyson.

PAT:

Nothing, Mr. Tennyson.

GRACE:

Nothing.

TENNYSON:

Don't you all have somewhere to be?

COLLEEN stares daggers at JESSIE.

Colleen?

COLLEEN:

I'm sure I do.

Beat.

JESSIE:

Come on, Pat. We don't want to be late for choir.

*JESSIE and PAT exit, PAT glancing back at
COLLEEN, still frozen in anger.*

TENNYSON:

Colleen.

GRACE:

Colleen was just... going to walk me to the art room. I forgot
where it is.

TENNYSON:

Alright, then. Go on.

*TENNYSON exits. COLLEEN finally lets out a
huge breath, part rage, part exhaustion.*

GRACE:

Colleen--?

*COLLEEN turns and stalks off, leaving GRACE
alone.*

6.

*The roof of the school. There is a lawn chair.
PARKER enters, with his backpack on. He sits
beside the lawn chair, takes out a paper bag
lunch. He removes a sandwich from the bag, and
begins to eat. There are sounds of pigeons.*

COLLEEN enters.

COLLEEN:

Hey.
Rough day today.

PARKER doesn't speak.

Rough day every day.

PARKER grunts.

You doing okay?

PARKER doesn't speak.

I need to sit down. Can you pull the chair over?

PARKER pulls the lawn chair over to
COLLEEN. She removes her arm crutches and
sits.

COLLEEN (cont):
These things get heavier every damn day.

PARKER:
I'm sorry.

COLLEEN:
Don't be.

PARKER:
I'm so—

COLLEEN:
Seriously, Parker. Seriously.

PARKER sits on the floor at her feet.

Look, Parker...

PARKER:
Yes.

COLLEEN:
This may not be a good time, but I'm not sure exactly when
a good time would be.
People are talking.

PARKER doesn't say anything.

They're seeing you... dive. A lot more frequently.

PARKER:
I have to find it.

COLLEEN:

Again?

PARKER:

Yes.

COLLEEN:

You're still searching for Atlantis.

PARKER:

Yes.

Beat.

COLLEEN:

You know it wasn't your fault, right? It was just something that happened. And it's okay. I'm okay.

Beat.

Parker... You need to face the possibility that you may never find Atlantis, buddy. That it might not... even exist. And if that's the case, are you going to keep diving? Or are you going to see what life is like up here? On the surface?

PARKER doesn't answer.

How's the sandwich?

PARKER:

It's ham and swiss.

COLLEEN:

I know. I made it.

PARKER:
I prefer salami.

COLLEEN:
We were out of salami. I'll go shopping on Saturday.

PARKER:
Can you get me chocolate milk?

COLLEEN:
Sure.
You can come with me, if you want.
You can come with me to the store, if you want.

PARKER:
Where do you suppose dad is right now?

COLLEEN:
Probably somewhere in the middle of the Goddamned Indian Ocean.

> *Beat.*

Tennyson is having us read *The Rime of the Ancient Mariner*.

PARKER:
"It is an ancient Mariner,
And he stoppeth one of three.
'By thy long grey beard and glittering eye,
Now wherefore stopp'st thou me?'"

COLLEEN:
You nerd.
Will you help me with it? Will you read it with me? Because English is not my best subject, and I made a promise to Briggs that I would... *apply* myself.

PARKER:
Sure.

COLLEEN:
Good. Because if there's one thing I can't stand, it's the freakin' ocean.

PARKER smiles. COLLEEN smiles.

Eat your sandwich.

The sound of cooing pigeons as the lights fade.

7.

Single spotlight up on JESSIE, near tears.

JESSIE:
I wasn't doing anything—I was minding my own business—and then she came at me with those, those, metal legs of hers, and she threatened to beat me with them. I told her that I would tell on her, but you know Colleen—she hasn't been herself since the accident, and then her grandparents' deaths —she's just a different girl. Darker. More violent. I wouldn't be at all surprised if she took out her rage and her frustrations on that poor disabled brother of hers. So I told her, leave me alone, Colleen, I only have the greatest respect for you! And do you know what she said?

Lights up on HENSON.

HENSON:
What did she say?

JESSIE:

She told me that I could go kill myself! Those were the exact words she used, Ms. Henson! She said: "You, Jessie, can go kill yourself. Now get out of here before I beat you senseless with my crutches."

HENSON:

It's worse than I thought.

JESSIE:

I know, right?

HENSON:

She actually said that?

JESSIE:

She screamed it at me. I was so afraid. I didn't know what to do. It was like the time Taylor ran into Nicki at the club and she was like, "what?" And then Nicki was like, "what?" And so I came to you.

HENSON:

You did the right thing, Jessie, you really did. Thank you for bringing this to my attention.

JESSIE:

And you won't tell Colleen that I told you?

HENSON:

Of course not—I prize confidentiality over everything. I promise, this will just remain between us.

JESSIE:

Thank you, Ms. Henson.

> *The light on JESSIE goes out, and HENSON's light is expanded to reveal PRINCIPAL*

*BRIGGS' office. TENNYSON is seated in the
chair.*

BRIGGS:
Calm down, Henson.

HENSON:
It's reached a critical mass, Principal Briggs. We know that Parker is disturbed—and is barely capable of functioning in this environment—

TENNYSON:
Parker aces every test, turns in every paper on time—

HENSON:
And how is his class participation, Mr. Tennyson?

TENNYSON:
The kid's a trauma victim—what do you expect his class participation to be?

HENSON:
Well, he may be a victim, but his sister has become a menace.

TENNYSON:
You really believe Jessie? That kid will say anything to get what she wants.

HENSON:
I believe Jessie over Colleen. Any day of the week!

BRIGGS:
Calm down, please, Ms. Henson.

TENNYSON:
Look, I'm no great champion of Colleen, but she is dealing with a ton of pressure—she's practically become Parker's parent. That girl has been dealt a terrible hand.

HENSON:
And now she's going to snap. We have to think of the other students in the school. Parker needs to go to a school where he can get the support he needs. And Colleen...

Pause.

BRIGGS:
Mr. Tennyson. Do you believe that Colleen has taken steps to change?

TENNYSON:
She came to me and apologized. She's promised to do the work. I... really can't answer beyond that.

HENSON:
If there is a possibility that Colleen has become physically violent, we need to call social services, Principal Briggs.

TENNYSON:
Is that really necessary?

BRIGGS:
If she is lashing out at the other students... it is.

Beat.

HENSON:
I'll call them right away.

HENSON exits.

TENNYSON:

That poor kid. Those poor kids.

BRIGGS:

What else could we do?
What choice do we have?

Lights fade on TENNYSON and BRIGGS.

8.

In the darkness, JUDY calls.

JUDY:

Parker? Parker!

DOUG's voice joins JUDY's.

DOUG:

Park! Hey buddy, please respond!

*Lights come up on JUDY and DOUG, they are
together, in rain slickers, and the sound of
thunder booms loudly overhead. Their voices are
periodically interrupted by static.*

JUDY:

The conditions up (*static*) are pretty terrible, P(*static*)—It's
seems probable that we lose (*static*) for a few minutes.

DOUG:

I'm going to (*static*) the communications equipment so it
(*static*) the signal to Petunia. Stand by, Pa(*static*)—

*A crack of thunder, a bolt of lightning, and then
the lights on JUDY and DOUG go black.*

Silence. Lights slowly come up on PARKER
inside Petunia. The sonar pings.)

PARKER:
Judy? Doug? Can you hear me? Can you hear me?

Beat. PARKER's anxiety begins to emerge, a
feeling he's never had in Petunia before. He tries
to shake it off.

I guess this will be a solo dive.

PARKER presses a few buttons, and the thrusters
activate. Their hum calms him.

From behind him, PARKER hears:

GRACE:
Hello?

PARKER freezes as GRACE appears at his side,
inside the cockpit of the submarine.

I'm... Grace.

PARKER remains frozen. The sonar pings.

So this is... this is your submarine?

PARKER:
(*hesitant*) Y-yes.

GRACE:
I'm Grace.

PARKER:
You said that.

                    Beat.

I'm Parker.

                    GRACE:
I know. I'm new here. At the school. And also here.

                    PARKER:
Ah.

                    GRACE:
Where are we?

                    PARKER:
(*slowly, PARKER's confidence begins to return*) According to
the coordinates, we are approximately two hundred twenty
miles off the coast of Southwest Morocco. Just past the
western most of the Canary Islands. La Palma.

                    GRACE:
What... what are we doing here?

                    PARKER:
There are some experts who postulate that this is where the
island of Atlantis was swallowed by the sea.

                    GRACE:
And that's what you're looking for? The Lost City of
Atlantis?

                    PARKER:
Yes.

GRACE:

Cool.

That was not the response PARKER was expecting.

And how deep are we?

PARKER:

About 7,000 feet and still descending.

GRACE:

Wow.
It's so dark down here.

PARKER:

The sun is a long way away.

A shadow passes over the sub, from left to right. The sub jostles.

Easy, Petunia.

GRACE:

Petunia?

PARKER:

That's her name.

GRACE:

What was that?

PARKER:

Probably a vampire squid. Although this is pretty far down, even for them.

GRACE:

Vampire squid?

PARKER:

Don't worry. They don't want anything to do with us.

Beat. Ping!

GRACE:

And once we find Atlantis. Once we get there. What's the plan?

PARKER:

The plan.
The people of Atlantis... do you know the story?

GRACE:

They were good and noble and then they fell. They were punished by the gods.

PARKER:

Exactly. And once we locate the city, we'll be able to search for some sign...

GRACE:

Of what?

PARKER:

Of whether they could be redeemed.

They descend in silence for a moment. It gets even darker around them.

GRACE:

You are very brave.

The sonar pings.

PARKER:

We've got something!

GRACE:

What is it?

*Shadows move across the stage, the darkened
shapes of fractured wood and broken masts.*

PARKER:

Shipwrecks. Dozens and dozens of shipwrecks.

GRACE:

These ships have to be two hundred, maybe three hundred
years old.

PARKER:

"Her beams bemocked the sultry main,
Like April hoar-frost spread;
But where the ship's huge shadow lay,
The charmèd water burnt away
A still and awful red."

GRACE:

We're reading that in Mr. Tennyson's class.

PARKER:

I know.

*A light flashes up on JUDY and DOUG, in the
midst of a powerful storm.*

JUDY:

Park(*static*)?

DOUG:

Come (*static*), Parker!

> *PARKER scrambles to adjust the intercom.*

PARKER:

Judy? Doug? Come in! Judy! Doug!

> *More static, and in another flash, JUDY and DOUG reappear...*

DOUG:

Parker, bud(*static*)—

> *...and vanish again.*

GRACE:

Should we go back?

PARKER:

No, we keep diving.

GRACE:

They sound like they're in trouble—

PARKER:

No! We keep diving! We have to keep diving!

> *COLLEEN's voice tears through the darkness, calling:*

COLLEEN:

Parker?

> *A third flash, and JUDY, COLLEEN, DOUG and then all at once:*

JUDY:

Park(*static*)

COLLEEN:

Parker!

DOUG:

(*static*)-ker! Come—

GRACE:

We have to go back—

PARKER:

We can't go back!

COLLEEN:

Goddamn it Park—

> *The lights burst on, full. PARKER has been*
> *ripped from his hallucination. He and GRACE*
> *are torn back into reality, and COLLEEN stands*
> *behind them, furious.*

What the hell was that?

> *PARKER stops—turns to COLLEEN.*

PARKER:

I'm so sorry, Coll. I'm so—

COLLEEN:

Stop it, Parker! Just stop it! All of it!

PARKER:

I'm—I'm sorry!

> *PARKER runs from the stage.*

GRACE:
(*calling after him*) Parker!

Beat.

COLLEEN:
I thought I told you to stay away from my brother.

GRACE:
I was only—

COLLEEN:
You were only *nothing*. How dare you feed into this, this *psychosis* of his! How dare you?

GRACE:
He was different in there, Colleen—he was a different person altogether! He was—

COLLEEN:
I don't want to hear your assessment of my brother's mental state or his personality or any of that garbage! I told you to stay away from him!

GRACE:
He's searching for something, Colleen—don't you see? Can't you see that?

COLLEEN:
What I *see* is that every day, I pick out his clothes and I cook his meals and I get him to school. Every day since we were left alone in that house, I am the only family he knows. I am the only one left to protect him!

GRACE:
Protect him? How is this protecting him?

COLLEEN:
What the hell do you know? He's my brother!

GRACE:
He's broken, Colleen!
When my mother died, I was broken, too. I was searching
for anything I could find that would bring me back, bring her
back. But it's not possible. You have to deal with it. He has
to deal with it. He has to.

COLLEEN stops, checks herself.

COLLEEN:
I didn't know your mother died.

GRACE:
She had cancer.
We moved here because my father needed to get us out of
the house. Everything reminded him of her.

COLLEEN:
I'm sorry, Grace.

GRACE:
Thank you.

Beat.

It's obvious that Parker has a lot he needs to work through.
And he needs you to help him work through it.

COLLEEN:
You don't even...

She sighs.

Parker had his first... *episode*... after the accident. He was in the hospital for a month. While he was gone, our *mother*— decided it was too much to handle. She dropped us with my grandparents and took off.

GRACE:

What about your dad?

COLLEEN:

My dad was out on a trawler off the coast of Greenland. He didn't even know she left him.

GRACE:

That's awful.

COLLEEN:

Last year, our grandparents died within, like hours of each other. Grandma had Alzheimer's—and Grandpa just... left with her. So Parker had another episode. But I didn't... I didn't want to call the hospital—I didn't want them to take him away. I didn't know if they would bring him back. And then I had to call the school and tell Principal Briggs what happened... The looks and the puppy-dog eyes and the comments behind my back—It just got to be... too much.

She pauses.

Last month—after another overdue bill and another Uber to the supermarket and another missed Skype call with my asshole father—I... lashed out. I blamed him. I shouldn't have, but I did.

GRACE:

Blamed him for what?

COLLEEN:
You name it, I blamed him for it.

Beat.

GRACE:
Do you still? Blame him, I mean?

COLLEEN:
It depends on the day.

GRACE:
I used to blame my mother. For leaving us. For dying on us.

COLLEEN:
When did you stop?

GRACE:
I don't know that I stopped.

Beat.

COLLEEN:
Ever since I lashed out, Parker's been having episodes left and right.

GRACE:
Have you spoken to a professional?

COLLEEN:
A therapist? Not since he was in the hospital.

GRACE:
Not for Parker. For *you*.

Beat.

COLLEEN:
I... I hadn't really thought about it.

GRACE:

And yeah, maybe for Parker, too.

COLLEEN:

Oh, God, I need a therapist.

GRACE:

It's not bad. I see one. Since mom got sick. She's a really nice lady.

COLLEEN:

I don't... I don't know...

GRACE:

It's just someone to talk to. Someone who can help you ask the questions you need to ask. That's it.

COLLEEN:

How would I... where would I even start to look?

PAT enters, nervous.

PAT:

Um, hey.

GRACE:

Hey, Pat.

PAT:

Colleen—I thought you should know.

COLLEEN:

Know what?

PAT:

I never—I never wanted anything to happen.

COLLEEN:
What? What's happening?

PAT:
I was just... I was angry. I was angry cause I thought we were friends. And you hurt me, and I guess I should have thought about how hurt you were feeling, but I didn't. I'm not always good at thinking about... stuff. So I'm, like, sorry for that.

COLLEEN:
That's... nice of you to say, Pat. But I don't understand...

GRACE:
Pat. What's going on?

PAT:
Jessie reported you to Ms. Henson. They've called the authorities. They're sending in someone from social services.

COLLEEN:
For Parker? They're going to take away Parker?

PAT:
For you, Colleen. They're coming for you, too.

Blackout.

9.

> *MR. ANKER, a cold, emotionless man dressed entirely in black, appears in a spotlight. He wears sunglasses indoors.*

ANKER:

Good morning. My name is Mr. Anker, and I'm from children's services. I'm going to need to ask you a series of questions.

A second spotlight comes up on COLLEEN, seated in a chair. She faces the audience, her crutches rest on her lap.

Name?

COLLEEN:

Colleen.

ANKER:

Can you speak up, please?

COLLEEN:

No.

A light comes up on JESSIE.

JESSIE:

My name is Jessie and I'm a junior and I love bicycling and watching horror movies where the hero dies a horrible death. My favorite colors are blue and magenta, and my favorite book has to be anything written in *Us Magazine* about celebrity breakups and celebrity hookups and celebrity culture. Do you want my 8 by 10?

ANKER:

I only asked you for your name.

JESSIE:

Weren't you listening?

Another light on GRACE.

GRACE:
Grace.

A final light on PAT.

PAT:
It's Pat. Actually, it's Patricia. Actually, it's Patricia Lee, but no one calls me Patricia Lee except my mom, and I hate it, so I usually just go by Pat. Or Patricia. Or Trisha. No one ever calls me "Sha."

ANKER:
O... kay.

A final light on PARKER, center—where the submarine would be.

PARKER sits in silence.

It's Parker, isn't it?

PARKER nods.

What grade are you in?

GRACE:
Junior.

PAT:
Junior.

JESSIE:
Eleventh.

COLLEEN:
None of your business.

ANKER:

Do you know why I'm here?

Across the stage, PRINCIPAL BRIGGS comes on, followed by a scattered—over-excited?—MS. HENSON, holding a cup of coffee. They stalk up to ANKER.

BRIGGS:

I will not have you disrupting my school more than it's already been disrupted, is that clear, Mr. Anker?

HENSON:

(*holding forth the cup*) Would you—

BRIGGS:

These students, the twins, have been traumatized enough over the last year.

HENSON:

(*holding forth the cup*) Can I offer you a—

BRIGGS:

There is still no evidence of any wrongdoing on behalf of Colleen, and I won't abide anyone jumping to conclusions about her level of responsibility until you've thoroughly investigated the matter. And I expect to be consulted before any decisions are final.

ANKER:

That's not how we operate, Principal Briggs.

BRIGGS:

That's how you're going to operate today, Mister Anker, or else my cousin in the mayor's office is going to be getting a call from me. Do I make myself clear?

HENSON:
(*holding forth the cup*) Can I interest you in a—

BRIGGS:
Henson, hurry up!

BRIGGS stalks off, HENSON follows.

ANKER:
Tell me about the incident.

PAT:
It was nothing really.

JESSIE:
It was terrible!

COLLEEN:
What incident?

ANKER:
Colleen threatened to assault you?

JESSIE:
Oh my God, yes—it was the worst. The absolute worst.
She's always had a temper on her, and I've known her since
before the—well, you know—she once pulled my hair in the
third grade and I've never forgotten it.

PAT:
Colleen was upset.

GRACE:
Jessie was goading her.

JESSIE:

She actually did assault me. She hit me in the leg with one of her crutches. She left a bruise. You can see it! You can see it right here! Can you see it?

PAT:

Jessie was being Jessie.

GRACE:

Just to get at Colleen.

JESSIE:

I had to go to the doctor. My mom said we might sue.

GRACE:

If I were Colleen, I would have been upset, too.

PAT:

Nobody meant it. What they said.

JESSIE:

For emotional distress, or something. I was emotional. I was distressed.

PAT:

We used to be friends, me and Colleen.

GRACE:

And poor Parker.

JESSIE:

She and that crazy brother of hers need to go. They're a menace!

> *Lights down on GRACE, JESSIE, and PAT, who exit.*

TENNYSON appears.

TENNYSON:
They are both bright—exceptionally bright. Parker's
writings read like he's already in college—and Colleen has
an aptitude for science that is incredible. But it doesn't
matter how smart they are. If you take the brightest kids in
the world and throw at them what life has thrown at Colleen
and Parker—what do you think will happen? They are kids
first, you know? They are teenagers first—with changing
bodies and forming brains and hormones and everything that
goes with it. We can't forget that they are children first. And
they are alone. You can't take them away from one another.
They are literally all the other has left.

TENNYSON vanishes.

ANKER:
Mr. Tennyson said you live alone.

COLLEEN:
No.

ANKER:
Sorry: You and Parker live alone.

COLLEEN:
By definition, that's not alone.

ANKER:
Your grandparents; they were scientists?

COLLEEN:
Grandma was a marine anthropologist. Grandpa designed
one of the first research submarines.

ANKER:

When did they die?

COLLEEN:

A year ago.

ANKER:

And your father?

COLLEEN:

He sent a bouquet of flowers from Borneo.

ANKER:

What does your father do?

COLLEEN:

He followed in the family business. He's a marine biologist.

ANKER:

And how often do you communicate with him?

COLLEEN:

Is there going to be a quiz on this?

ANKER:

Can we talk about your father?

COLLEEN:

I have nothing to say.

ANKER:

When was the last time you spoke with your father?

COLLEEN:
What do you want me to say? Alright? I take care of Parker
—I've always taken care of him, even though I'm literally
four minutes younger than he is. When he needs shoes, I buy
them. When he needs food, I feed him. Our grandparents left
us a house with a mortgage and electrical bills and a clogged
bathroom sink, and my father is off playing underwater
Indiana Jones eleven months out of the year. Is it ideal? No,
but it's the way we are operating right now. And yeah,
maybe we're not doing everything perfectly, but we're doing
pretty good for the crappy hand we were dealt. We have
problems, and we're working on them. Do you understand
me? We're working on them! I'm working on them.
I'm figuring out how to work on them.

ANKER:
You didn't answer my question, Colleen. When was the last
time you spoke to your father?

> *Frustrated, COLLEEN exits. PARKER is alone*
> *on the stage with MR. ANKER.*

Parker?
When was the last time?

> *MR. ANKER begins to fade away, his voice*
> *getting further and further, as if under water.*

Parker?
Parker?

10.

> *The ping of the sonar, the whir of the engines.*
> *PARKER is inside Petunia, descending,*

descending. The ocean around him is pitch black. He speaks softly.

PARKER:

This is the last place left to search, the last possible location of the lost city of Atlantis: the sea floor of Antarctica. The bottom of the ocean at the bottom of the map. I've looked... everywhere else. I've followed all the clues, all the legends, all the myths. We are nearing the ocean floor at 20,000 feet, and I am concerned about the sharp drop in temperature since we left the waters south of Australia.

He listens to the movement of Petunia in the water.

I... lost contact with Judy and Doug hours ago. Maybe it's been days. I can't really tell. And my oxygen levels... are low.

If I don't find it. If I don't find it here... I don't know what I'll do.

He stops. He is in despair.

"I moved, and could not feel my limbs:
I was so light—almost
I thought that I had died in sleep,
And was a blessed ghost."

Beat.

It's... cold.

The sonar pings.

From a distance, a voice—COLLEEN's voice— echoes in the deep.

COLLEEN:

(*offstage*) Parker!

> *PARKER shakes his head. He doesn't want to hear it.*

(*offstage*) Parker, can you hear me?

> *Pressing a few buttons, the whir of Petunia's engines get louder.*

> *COLLEEN enters behind him.*

Parker?

> *For a moment, the world flashes, the real world lights ignite, and then fade back into the depths of the ocean as COLLEEN is transported to the helm of Petunia, beside her brother.*

PARKER:

What do you want?

> *COLLEEN is a little stunned.*

COLLEEN:

Is this... is this...?

PARKER:

This is the ocean, Coll.

COLLEEN:

It's so... big.

> *PARKER shoots her a look.*

COLLEEN (cont):
I mean, I know the ocean is big—but it feels so... huge. And
empty.

PARKER:
Not always.

COLLEEN:
How did it go? With that guy?

PARKER:
What guy?

COLLEEN:
From social services.

PARKER:
They can't take me away.

COLLEEN:
Right. Right!

PARKER:
Not yet.

COLLEEN:
Not *ever*, Park. Not ever.

PARKER:
Not until I find it.

COLLEEN:
Find what?

PARKER:
Atlantis! Not until I find the Lost City!

COLLEEN:
We've talked about this—we have spent hours talking about
this—there is no—

PARKER:
There is! There has to be.

COLLEEN:
Why, Park? Why does there have to be?

PARKER:
Because I need to fix them.

COLLEEN:
Who?

PARKER:
The Atlanteans. The people who fell. If I can figure out how
to fix them...

COLLEEN:
Then what?

PARKER:
Then I can figure out how to fix me.

Beat.

COLLEEN:
Do you think... do you think you're being punished for
being... evil?

PARKER:
I pushed you, Colleen.
I pushed you off that roof.
We were playing, and we were joking, and in the back of my
mind, I thought, what if? What if I just reached out and...?

Beat.

What I did was unforgivable.

COLLEEN:
I don't know.

PARKER:
I need to figure out how to redeem them.

COLLEEN:
Parker—
You can start by redeeming me.

PARKER:
You?

COLLEEN:
I'm angry, Park. I'm angry all the time. And I'm afraid. I'm afraid that they're going to separate us or send us away. I'm afraid dad is never going to come home. I'm afraid we're going to lose the house. I'm afraid we're going to lose each other.
I need you to help me, buddy. I need you to help me figure things out. Not down here, not in the ocean. Up there. In real life. I need you to help me work through all this *garbage* I'm feeling. All the anger, all the guilt, all the shame and the embarrassment and the hurt.
I know you feel the same way.

PARKER:
Yeah.

COLLEEN:
So let's help each other. Let's find a doctor.
Let's figure this out and get on with our lives.

A ping from the sonar, and PARKER looks out into the sea.

PARKER:

We're nearing the ocean floor.

COLLEEN:

How the heck can you tell?

From the intercom, static, and then:

JUDY:

Parker? Parker!

Lights come up on JUDY, dressed in heavy winter apparel.

Oh, I'm so glad we were finally able to get the communications link back open!

Lights come up on DOUG, similarly clothed.

DOUG:

Jeez, kiddo, where the hell have you been?

PARKER:

Judy! Doug!

COLLEEN:

Grandma? Grandpa?

JUDY:

Hello, Colleen, sweetie. So nice of you to take this dive with your brother.

COLLEEN:

Wait—what—how—?

DOUG:

Is she having a stroke?

PARKER:

I don't think so.

DOUG:

Good. It'd be a bitch to get a medical crew down there.
What's your status, buddy?

PARKER:

It looks we're coming around the western edge of the
continent.

JUDY:

If the entrance is going to be anywhere, it's going to be
where the Antarctic Peninsula connects with the mainland,
beneath the Larsen Ice Shelf.

PARKER:

Engaging thrusters.

The sound of the thrusters grows louder.

COLLEEN:

What exactly are we looking for?

JUDY:

Streets, statues, temples—there's got to be something left
standing after five thousand years of oceanic burial.

PARKER:

Doug?

DOUG:
Look, even if the ancient Atlanteans were wiped out with a nuclear blast, you'll be able to find something. A pillar, a post—something.

PARKER:
Colleen—turn on the forward searchlights.

COLLEEN:
Where?

PARKER:
The yellow switch.

COLLEEN does so. A light bursts on upstage, and GRIGGS and HENSON appear.

GRIGGS:
Mister Anker has rejected the complaint, Colleen—although he did suggest you two get some additional counseling—and not with Ms. Henson.

HENSON:
We've spoken to Patrick and Grace and found out what really happened between you and Jessie, Colleen. I'm... sorry if we—if I—jumped to conclusions.

GRIGGS:
And after several attempts, we were finally able to get in touch with your father. He'll be heading back to the states within the week. He had no idea all of this was going on. Did you know he has been examining sea slugs in Madagascar?

They fade away.

PARKER:

The temperature may be affecting the wiring. Turn them off and try again.

A second burst of light, PAT stands in it.

PAT:

I want to try again, Colleen. I can be a better friend. To you and to Parker. And I think you need all the friends you can get.

The light fades, as does PAT.

DOUG:

I'll run a full diagnostic as soon as you get topside.

PARKER:

That's not going to help us now.

She tries again; another; TENNYSON appears.

TENNYSON:

Your paper on maritime themes in Romantic poetry was the best I've read, Colleen. If you continue to do work this solid for the rest of the semester, you should be able to get a passing mark. But tell me—are you sure you didn't go to your brother for help on this?

He fades.

PARKER:

Try the lights on the arms.

Another flash, revealing GRACE.

GRACE:

I know what it's like to be angry. I know what it's like to be sad. I wouldn't want to see anyone go through what you are both going through. But you don't have to do it alone anymore. I'll help you. We'll all help you.

JUDY:

Parker, Colleen—try lighting up the whole array at once.

> *A final blast of light, and the ocean opens up to reveal golds, blues, pinks, whites, shimmering around them.*

COLLEEN:

Parker—is that—?

PARKER:

Oh my God.

COLLEEN:

Parker... it's...

COLLEEN and PARKER:

Atlantis.

JUDY:

You found it.

DOUG:

I knew you could do it, buddy.

COLLEEN:

It's beautiful.

JUDY:

Of course it is.

PARKER:

It's... it's *glorious*.

> *COLLEEN reaches out, and takes her brother's hand. PARKER holds back tears.*

JUDY:

It was always going to be, sweetie.

> *JUDY vanishes.*

COLLEEN:

I almost wish we could get out... and touch it.

DOUG:

You can, Petunia. You can.

> *DOUG vanishes, and as he goes, the submarine evaporates around PARKER and COLLEEN. They stand on the ocean floor, staring up at the majestic sight of the Lost City of Atlantis, stretching out for miles and miles before them.*

PARKER:

Shall we get closer?

COLLEEN:

Together, Parker.

PARKER:

Together, Colleen.
We'll swim.
Let's swim.

> *PARKER gently takes COLLEEN's crutches, lays them behind them on the ocean floor. Then he reaches over, and offering a helping hand, both*

of them float up up up, and into the city in the sea.

Lights fade to black.

END OF PLAY